ENDANGERED ANIMALS OF
NORTH AMERICA

WORLD
BOOK

a Scott Fetzer company
Chicago
worldbook.com

Staff

Executive Committee

President
Donald D. Keller
Vice President and Editor in Chief
Paul A. Kobasa
Vice President, Sales
Sean Lockwood
Vice President, Finance
Anthony Doyle
Director, Marketing
Nicholas A. Fryer
Director, Human Resources
Bev Ecker

Editorial

Associate Director,
Annuals and Topical Reference
Scott Thomas
Managing Editor,
Annuals and Topical Reference
Barbara A. Mayes
Senior Editor,
Annuals and Topical Reference
Christine Sullivan
Manager, Indexing Services
David Pofelski
Administrative Assistant
Ethel Matthews
Manager, Contracts & Compliance
(Rights & Permissions)
Loranne K. Shields

Editorial Administration

Senior Manager, Publishing
Operations
Timothy Falk

Manufacturing/ Production

Director
Carma Fazio
Manufacturing Manager
Sandra Johnson
Production / Technology
Manager
Anne Fritzinger
Proofreader
Nathalie Strassheim

Graphics and Design

Art Director
Tom Evans
Senior Designer
Don Di Sante
Media Researcher
Jeff Heimsath
Manager, Cartographic Services
Wayne K. Pichler
Senior Cartographer
John M. Rejba

Marketing

Marketing Specialists
Alannah Sharry
Annie Suhy
Digital Marketing Specialists
Iris Liu
Nudrat Zoha

Writer

A. J. Smuskiewicz

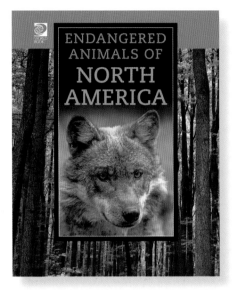

The cover image is the endangered red wolf.

World Book, Inc.
233 North Michigan Avenue
Chicago, Illinois 60601 U.S.A.

For information about other World Book publications, visit our website at **www.worldbook.com** or call **1-800-WORLDBK (967-5325).**
For information about sales to schools and libraries, call 1-800-975-3250 (United States) or 1-800-837-5365 (Canada).

Library of Congress Cataloging-in-Publication Data

Endangered animals of North America.
    pages cm. -- (Endangered animals of the world)
    Includes index.
    Summary: "Information about some of the more important and interesting endangered animals of North America, including the animal's common name, scientific name, and conservation status; also includes a map showing the range of each animal featured; and a glossary, additional resources, and an index"-- Provided by publisher.
    ISBN 978-0-7166-5625-8
    1. Endangered species--North America--Juvenile literature. I. World Book, Inc.
QL84.E53 2014
591.68097--dc23
                                    2014020174

Endangered Animals of the World
ISBN: 978-0-7166-5620-3 (set)

Printed in China by Shenzhen Donnelley Printing Co., Ltd. Guangdong Province
1st printing October 2014

Contents

Why species in North America are threatened

Threats to wildlife in North America are largely related to human activities. Loss of natural *habitats* (the type of environment in which an organism lives) has been widespread. This loss has resulted from *urbanization* (the growth and spread of cities), *agricultural development* (the replacement of natural land with farmland), industrialization and pollution, and the construction of roads, highways, dams. In addition, excessive hunting and fishing have brought many *species* to the brink of extinction. (A species is a group of animals or plants that have certain permanent characteristics in common and are able to interbreed.)

An estimated 2,300 species in North America are threatened, many critically. Of course, this number includes only those species known to science. Many species remain undiscovered. And almost certainly, a number of these animals are in peril or have even disappeared.

North America's natural places remained free of harmful human influences longer than most other places. Although Native Americans lived on the continent for thousands of years, these *aboriginal* people (the earliest people present in a region) changed the natural environment very little. They lacked the technology to seriously harm the environment, and they had a deep respect for nature ingrained in their culture.

Europeans began to colonize North America in the 1500's. As they spread across the continent, they cut down forests and turned prairies into farms. They replaced native species of plants and animals with foreign species. And they hunted and killed vast numbers of native animals.

During the 1800's, industrialization spread across the continent. Railroads crossed the landscape. Factories polluted the air and water. When automobiles became popular in the early 1900's, more pollution entered the environment. These changes altered *ecosystems* so much that many plants and animals could not survive. (An ecosystem is made up of living organisms and their physical environment.)

By the 1960's, Americans were increasingly aware of the harm they were causing to wildlife. Scientists warned that hundreds of North American plant and animal species were in danger of becoming extinct.

In 1973, the U.S. Congress passed the Endangered Species Act (ESA). The ESA is designed to protect threatened species and their habitats. Once a species is classified as *Endangered* (in danger of extinction throughout all or much of its *range* [natural area]) or *Threatened* (likely to become endangered within the foreseeable future), that species and its habitat fall under federal protection.

In this volume. The species presented in this volume represent a variety of endangered animals in North America. From the smallest and simplest to the largest and most powerful, the continent's wildlife is facing challenges from human beings.

Scientific sequence. Species are presented in a standard scientific sequence that goes from simple to complex: from insects or other *invertebrates* (anmals without backbones), through fish, amphibians, reptiles, birds, and mammals.

Range. Red areas on maps indicate an animal's range on the North American continent.

Glossary: Italicized words, except for scientific names, appear with their definitions in the Glossary at the end of the book.

Conservation status. Each species discussed in this book is listed with its common name, scientific name, and conservation status. The conservation status tells how seriously a species is threatened. Unless noted differently, the status is according to the International Union for Conservation of Nature (IUCN), a global organization of conservation groups. The most serious IUCN status is *Extinct,* followed by *Extinct in the Wild, Critically Endangered, Endangered, Vulnerable, Near Threatened,* and *Least Concern. Criteria* (rules) used to determine these conservation statuses are included in the list on the right.

Some status designations are according to the United States Fish and Wildlife Service (USFWS), as indicated by the species's name. Some statuses are according to the Committee on the Status of Endangered Wildlife in Canada (COSEWIC). Organizations use different criteria when making their classifications.

Conservation statuses

Extinct All individuals of the species have died

Extinct in the Wild The species is no longer observed in its past range

Critically Endangered The species will become extinct unless immediate conservation action is taken

Endangered The species is at high risk of becoming extinct due to a large decrease in range, population, or both

Vulnerable The species is at some risk of becoming extinct due to a moderate decrease in range, population, or both

Near Threatened The species is likely to become threatened in the future

Least Concern The species is common throughout its range

Icons. The icons indicate various threats that have made animals vulnerable to extinction.

Key to icons

 Disease

 Global warming

 Habitat disturbance

 **Habitat loss**

Hunting

Pollution

Ranching

Scaphirhynchus albus

Conservation status: Endangered (IUCN & USFWS)

Sturgeons are large, primitive-looking fishes with tough skin covered in rows of bony plates (instead of the scales that most fish have). They have long, flat snouts with whiskerlike growths, called barbels, in front of the mouth. The tooth-less mouth, at the bottom of the snout, is used to suck up small fish, crustaceans, worms, insect *larvae* (immature forms), and other animals that live on the river bottom. Sturgeons look primitive because they belong to an ancient group of fish that have changed little since the time of the dinosaurs. Fossils of sturgeon ancestors have been found that are more than 150 million years old—from the Jurassic Period.

Species. The pallid sturgeon is similar and closely related to another *species* (type) that exists today—shovelnose sturgeon. The shovelnose sturgeon is typically smaller and brownish in color, while the pallid sturgeon is grayish-white. The pallid sturgeon can grow to a length of about 6 feet (1.8 meters) and weigh as much as 80 pounds (36 kilograms).

Reproduction. Pallid sturgeons become sexually mature at 7 to 15 years old. Some females may *spawn* (lay eggs) only once every 10 years. However, the fish can live longer than most fish. Scientists know that some pallid sturgeons have lived for as long as 50 years.

Habitat. The favorite *habitat* (living place) of pallid sturgeons consists of large, deep river channels—especially channels in which the water flows quickly and strongly over a sand or gravel bed. The water in their streams is usually *turbid* (cloudy and murky) with *silt* (tiny pieces of sand or clay floating in water). These fish are most common in the main channels of the lower Mississippi River and the upper Missouri River. Their *range* (natural area) extends from Montana to Louisiana.

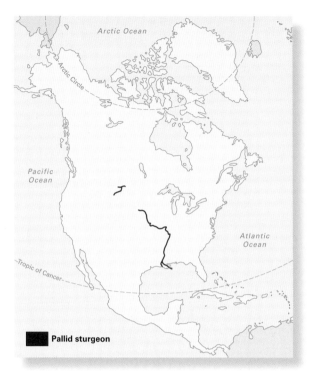

Pallid sturgeon

Threats. The pallid sturgeon faces a high risk of extinction, mainly because of harmful changes to its habitat caused by people. Many of the sturgeon's natural homes—rivers—have been altered by dams, canals, or other types of construction. For example, the building of a large dam may turn a river into a lake, which is not a suitable habitat for this species. Certain other activities of people have affected the temperature, turbidity, or water level of the sturgeon's rivers. Such changes are stressful and potentially fatal to the fish.

Industrial and agricultural pollution has contaminated many parts of the sturgeon's range. Commercial fishing has reduced some of the sturgeon's supply of prey.

Still another threat to the pallid sturgeon as a species is mating with shovelnose sturgeons. Such crossbreeding produces offspring that are *hybrids* (mixes) of the two species. Biologists are not sure how many pure pallid sturgeons remain in the wild, but most estimates place the number between 10,000 and 20,000.

The pallid sturgeon is a primitive-looking fish (right) that is covered in bony plates, instead of the scales typical of most fish.

A state conservation official releases young pallid sturgeons (below) in an attempt to restock the Missouri River in Montana.

Cryptobranchus alleganiensis

Conservation status: Near Threatened (IUCN) Endangered (USFWS)

The hellbender is the largest salamander in North America, reaching a length as great as 20 inches (50 centimeters). This amphibian has a flattened body that is covered with very slimy, loose, wrinkly skin. Its eyes are tiny and have no lids. These animals may be greenish, yellowish brown, or grayish in color, with black spots scattered across the body.

Habitat. Hellbenders live in large streams and rivers with cold, fast-flowing water. They are often found hiding under large rocks. Small, isolated populations of this *species* (type) occur in waters from New York south to Alabama and Mississippi and west to Arkansas and

■ Hellbender

Missouri. According to the IUCN, the overall North American population of the hellbender is classified as "Near Threatened." However, the population in the Ozarks region—an area of hills, lakes, and rivers that includes the southern part of Missouri and parts of northern Arkansas—is classified as "Endangered" according to the USFWS. In other words, the Ozarks population—found in the Spring River and White River systems—is the most endangered group of hellbender.

The Ozarks population has declined by about 75 percent since the 1980's. Fewer than 600 hellbenders may survive in the wilds of the Ozarks today, according to a number of estimates.

Threats. Loss of *habitat* (living place) is the main reason that the hellbender population in the Ozarks is endangered. This species tends to be very sensitive to any kind of environmental change in its habitat.

In some parts of the Ozarks, floods may have wiped out certain populations. Pollution from agricultural chemicals, sewage treatment systems, and ore and gravel mining operations has also played an important role in the problem of population decline.

Chemical pollution is especially dangerous to the eggs and aquatic *larvae* (immature forms) of hellbenders. Furthermore, logging activities have led to increased *sediment* (loose dirt) flowing from the land into rivers. The sediment settles at the bottom of the rivers and covers the rocks and gravel that the amphibians use for nesting.

Another problem for the hellbender's river habitat is the building of dams to create hydroelectric power plants and lakes for boating and swimming. While useful to people, these facilities destroy the fast-flowing streams and rivers that the hellbenders need to survive.

Some recreational fishers kill hellbenders whenever they happen to come across them, because they incorrectly believe that the amphibians are dangerously poisonous to people and that the hellbenders kill game fish and eat fish eggs.

Conservation. Scientists are attempting to boost the hellbender population of the Ozarks by breeding the amphibians in captivity. For example, the St. Louis Zoo and the Missouri Department of Conservation are breeding hellbenders with the intention of later releasing them into the wild.

Breeding the animals in captivity ensures that they at least survive the dangerous period when they are young and small—a time when they are most likely to be killed by predators.

The hellbender, the largest salamander in North America, is threatened by pollution of its habitat, particularly from agricultural runoff and logging.

Crocodylus acutus

Conservation status: Vulnerable (IUCN) Endangered in most areas/Threatened in Florida (USFWS)

Crocodiles are known for their massive, powerful jaws equipped with numerous long, sharp teeth. They use these strong, snapping jaws to catch a variety of animals, from fish and turtles to such mammals as muskrats and even deer. A croc handles a large animal by first seizing the animal with its jaws and then twisting and spinning the animal in the water until the body breaks into smaller pieces. Even people, especially children, may not be safe if they get too close to the water. Crocodiles are more likely than alligators to attack people.

Habitat. The American crocodile lives in rivers, marshes, and swamps in southern Florida and in *brackish* (partly salty) water along the state's southern coast, as well as in the West Indies and Central America. The USFWS classifies this *species* (type) as "Threatened" in Florida and "Endangered" everywhere else. The IUCN classifies the species as "Vulnerable." American crocodiles grow to an average length of 11.5 feet (3.5 meters), though some males may be more than 19.7 feet (6 meters) long.

Crocodiles are much more than just awesome killing machines. These reptiles are highly specialized for living in water. The crocodile's eyes, ears, and nostrils are all on top of its head, allowing it to breathe and see its above-water surroundings while keeping the rest of its body submerged. A croc can see what's going on underwater by covering its eyes with a clear "third eyelid." And a flap of skin that closes the windpipe allows the crocodile to open its mouth underwater to catch prey without drowning.

Reproduction. Female crocodiles lay their eggs on land and cover them with sand. They guard the nest until the eggs hatch in about 90 days. The mother and father sometimes help the hatchlings break through the eggshells. Both

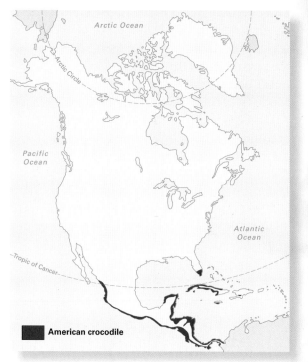

American crocodile

parents may watch over the baby crocs to protect them against raccoons and other predators.

Threats. Crocodiles have long been hunted for their scaly, attractive hides, which are made into leather for shoes, handbags, belts, and other products. Hunting caused populations of the American crocodile to fall to dangerous levels by the 1960's. The reptiles were also killed for meat and sport, and some accidentally drowned when they became caught in fishing gear. In Florida, much crocodile *habitat* (living place) has been lost to *urban* (city) developments, especially in the areas of Miami and the Florida Keys.

Conservation. Laws have forbidden the hunting of American crocodiles since the 1970's. As a result, their population is now increasing in Florida. Some lost habitat has been replaced by artificial nesting sites created by conservationists just for crocodiles. In addition, biologists sometimes collect crocodile eggs and hatch them in incubators, safely returning the young to the wild after they are able to take care of themselves.

The American crocodile eats most of its prey whole.

Culebra Island giant anole

Anolis roosevelti

Conservation status: Critically Endangered (IUCN) Endangered (USFWS)

The Culebra Island giant anole *species* (type) of large lizard may or may not be extinct. Despite repeated scientific surveys, biologists have not reported seeing one since the 1930's. At that time, it was known to live on islands in the eastern Caribbean Sea, including Isla Culebra, Puerto Rico, and the Virgin Islands. If the Culebra Island giant anole still exists, biologists suspect there may be fewer than 50 individuals.

The Culebra Island giant anole was first scientifically described in 1931 by U.S. Army Major Chapman Grant, a grandson of President Ulysses S. Grant. The scientific name of the species, *Anolis roosevelti,* was dedicated to Theodore Roosevelt, Jr., then governor of Puerto Rico and a son of President Theodore Roosevelt. Major Grant later helped found the Herpetologists' League, an international organization that studies amphibians and reptiles. This organization also works for the conservation of amphibians and reptiles.

Appearance. Because a living Culebra Island giant anole has not been found for so long, most of what biologists know about the species comes from preserved specimens in museums. Based on these specimens, biologists believe that the body of the giant anole ranges from 5.5 to 6.3 inches (14 to 16 centimeters) in length, not counting a tapered tail that brings the total length to more than 15 inches (38 centimeters). Like other kinds of anoles, the Culebra Island giant has a baggy throat flap called a dewlap. The male's dewlap is large and colorful. He fans it back and forth to attract females or to scare away other males.

Habitat. Giant anoles are *arboreal* (living in trees). They climb through trees and shrubs in search of insects, fruits, and other food. These lizards are excellent climbers—thanks to the wide fleshy pad and sharp claw on each toe. The pad has thousands of hairlike bristles that help the foot stick to tree bark.

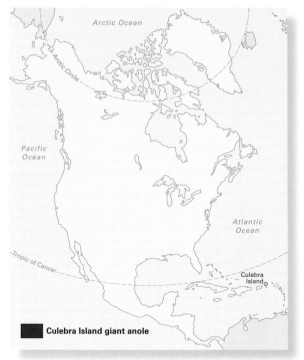

Culebra Island giant anole

Threats. Most of the forests on the Caribbean islands on which the giant anole was known to have lived in the 1930's have been destroyed. The loss of these forest *habitats* (living places) is the main reason for the anole's rarity—or extinction. Another problem is the widespread grazing of livestock on the islands. Grazing by cattle and other domestic animals has further reduced the natural plant cover needed by the anoles. Other factors that have harmed the natural habitat of the giant anole have been the growth of *urban* (city) areas—with their homes and businesses—and the spread of tourism. Many tourists who visit natural areas harm those areas by collecting or trampling on plants, leaving litter and garbage, and other careless actions.

Conservation. Conservationists are trying to determine if the Culebra Island giant anole still exists. Some conservationists think it might be found in remote places on some of the region's smaller islands. If it is found, scientists will need to set up and manage new protected areas for the species.

The Culebra Island giant anole (above, in a museum display) is a large lizard native to Isla Culebra (background) and other islands in the eastern Caribbean. A living Culebra anole has not been seen since the 1930's.

Gopher tortoise

Gopherus polyphemus

Conservation status: Vulnerable (IUCN)
Threatened (USFWS)

The big, blunt head of the gopher tortoise sticks out from under a brown or tan *carapace* (upper shell) that is from 4.3 to 9.4 inches (11 to 24 centimeters) long. Its front feet are strong and built like shovels, making it easy for the reptile to dig long, deep burrows into the ground.

Habitat. The gopher tortoise lives in sandy ridges and longleaf pine forests in the southeastern United States. Its *range* (natural area) extends from South Carolina southward into Florida and westward into Louisiana.

Burrows. The gopher tortoise's burrows are very important for both its behavior and the local *ecosystem* (natural system made up of living organisms and their physical environment). It sleeps in its burrows at night and comes out during the day to feed on grasses, berries, and other low-growing plant food. Each tortoise digs several burrows throughout its home area. These burrows may eventually be used by many other kinds of animals besides the tortoises, including frogs, snakes, raccoons, opossums, and burrowing owls. Some of these other animals are endangered *species* (types). So the survival of these species may depend on the survival of the gopher tortoise.

The burrows are also import hiding places during fires. But natural forest fires benefit the tortoises by clearing away old, thick shrub and tree growth and letting more sunshine reach the ground and the plants they depend on for food.

Lifespan. Many animals—including armadillos, foxes, opossums, raccoons, and skunks—like to eat the small, young tortoises. If the young reptiles are lucky enough to make it to adulthood, they may live long lives. Gopher tortoises are known to live for more than 40 years in the wild. In the safety of captivity, some individuals have even lived for more than 80 years.

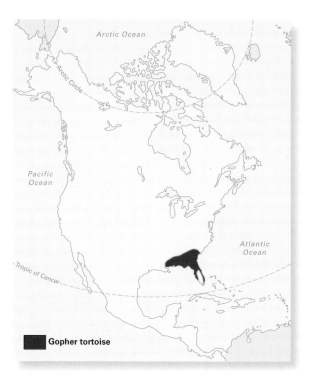

Gopher tortoise

Threats. Gopher tortoise populations have been broken up and isolated from each other by *urban* (city) and *agricultural developments* (including citrus farms) and by mining activities (particularly for phosphate, a mineral used in agriculture and industry). Roads, buildings, dams, and other structures destroy the tortoises' natural *habitat* (living place) and make it impossible for them to spread to new areas. Some people hunt the tortoises illegally for food or for pets. Some local populations of gopher tortoises have been hunted to extinction.

Conservation and antihunting laws are helping to protect gopher tortoises. In some cases, scientists have relocated, or moved, the tortoises to new locations when their original homes were threatened by human development. Better habitat protection is the best way to protect the gopher tortoise.

The gopher tortoise is native to the longleaf pine forests of the Southeastern United States. Antihunting laws have been passed to protect it.

Mona boa
Epicrates monensis monensis
Conservation status: Threatened (USFWS)

Virgin Islands tree boa
Epicrates monensis granti (USFWS)
Conservation status: Endangered

Both Mona and Virgin Island tree boas have a similar appearance, with dark brown blotches outlined in black and separated by a light brown background. These snakes grow to an average length of about 31 inches (80 centimeters). Compared with other kinds of boas, they are small. Females are larger than males.

Species. These two subspecies of snake together make up a single *species* (type) of tree boa that lives on islands in the Caribbean Sea. The Mona subspecies lives on Isla Mona (an island west of Puerto Rico) as well as on Puerto Rico itself. The Virgin Islands sub–species is found on several of the British and United States Virgin Islands.

Habitat. As they slither through the moist woodlands and forests of their subtropical island homes, the tree boas hunt for small animal prey. Their most common food is an interesting little lizard known as the crested anole. Like a chameleon, the crested anole can change its color—from red to brown to gray to black—based on the air temperature, its surroundings, and whatever behavior it is engaged in. The tree boas also eat birds—especially nestlings found in trees—and mice and other small mammals.

Reproduction. As is the case with all kinds of tree boas, the Mona and Virgin Islands subspecies are *viviparous* (the young develop inside the mother's body, much as young mammals do). This reproduction method stands in contrast to the usual reptile method of reproduction, in which the mother lays eggs outside her body. The young tree boas develop inside the mother

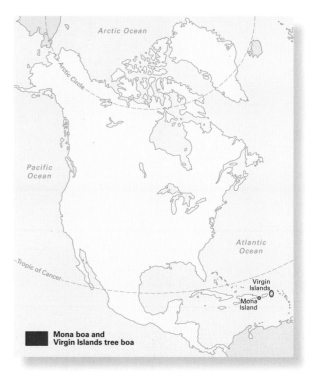

Mona boa and
Virgin Islands tree boa

Both the Virgin Islands boa (left) and the Mona boa (above) are native to islands of the eastern Caribbean.

for about 130 days. They grow quickly after birth. The boas may become sexually mature—capable of mating and having their own young—within two years.

Threats. The natural forest *habitats* (living places) of the Mona and Virgin Island tree boas have been greatly disturbed by human activities. The main problem has been the introduction by people of mammal predators to the islands.

Nonnative killers—especially *feral* cats (escaped domestic cats), black rats, and Indian mongoose—have found the tree boas to be easy prey. Domestic goats and pigs also sometimes kill the snakes.

Other human activities that have reduced the snakes' populations include the spread of cities, farms, and logging—all of which wipe out natural areas on the islands.

In addition, such extreme storms as hurricanes, fairly common in the region, and flooding have harmed the boa populations. Many scientists believe that such extreme weather events are becoming more common because of human-related *climate change* (long-term changes in the climate believed to be caused mainly by the burning of fossil fuels).

Conservation. Biologists and other scientists are working to protect both the endangered Mona and Virgin Island tree boas. They are breeding the snakes in captivity and releasing the young in protected sites. They are setting up new protected sites, and they are trying to get rid of nonnative predators.

Gymnogyps californianus

Conservation status: Critically Endangered (IUCN) Endangered (USFWS)

The California condor is North America's largest flying land bird—that is, a bird that does not live at sea. Its wingspan may stretch for 9.5 feet (2.9 meters). The bird may weigh as much as 23 pounds (10.4 kilograms). Most of this big bird's feathers are black, except for the white on the underside of the wings. Its mostly featherless neck and head are reddish-orange and surrounded by a fluffy collar of black feathers.

California condors are amazingly powerful and graceful fliers. They can soar and glide for vast distances over open, hilly country, typically flapping their wings only once an hour. With their sharp vision, they scan the ground for food as they fly. Like other kinds of vultures, condors eat *carrion* (the remains of dead animals).

California condors have an unusual way of cooling themselves when they get too hot. In this method—called *urohydrosis*—the birds urinate on their own legs. As the urine evaporates into the air, it carries away heat from the body. This may seem strange, but it is actually similar to the way people cool themselves through the evaporation of sweat.

Habitat. When not flying or eating, California condors like to rest on rocky cliffs and other high perches. The *species* (type) used to live in many parts of western North America.

Reproduction. Females lay their eggs among boulders or inside caves or open spaces in the ground. A female condor can lay only one egg every two years. This means that the species reproduces slowly. So its population will take a long time to recover from its endangered status.

Threats. Once widespread, the California condor was almost extinct by the early 1980's, when only 22 of the birds were known to have survived in the wild. Large numbers of California condors had been shot by people who

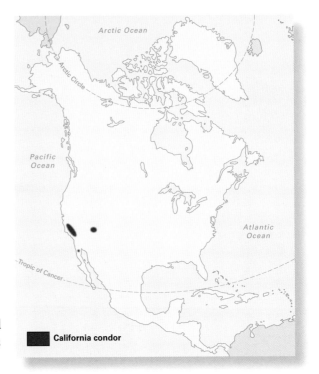

California condor

saw them as dangerous animals or omens of bad luck. Others died from lead poisoning after eating dead animals that had been shot with lead bullets. Still others died from eating poisoned *carcasses* (dead bodies of animals) set out by ranchers to kill coyotes. Some died from colliding with electric power lines. Many California condors died as their natural open *habitat* (living place) was transformed into crowded cities, farmland, roads, and other human developments.

Conservation. In 1982, scientists began an ambitious program to capture all wild California condors and build up their numbers in captivity. The scientists caught the last wild condor in 1987. Since that time, several hundred condors have been born and raised in captivity. Biologists began releasing some of these birds into the wild in 1992—including in California's Los Padres National Forest, in Arizona's Grand Canyon National Park, and in the Sierra de San Pedro Martir in Baja California, Mexico. There are now roughly 200 California condors back in the wild.

The California condor is North America's largest flying land bird, with a wingspread of up to 9.5 feet (2.9 meters).

Grus americana

Conservation status: Endangered (IUCN, COSEWIC & USFWS)

Standing as tall as 5 feet (1.5 meters), the long-legged, long-necked whooping crane is the tallest bird in North America. These striking birds are all white except for black tips on the wings, a black mask around the eyes, and a red patch on the head. The "whoopers" get their name from their loud, buglelike calls.

Habitat and threats. Many thousands of whooping cranes used to nest throughout the north-central United States and Canada, with a separate group living year-round in Louisiana. These huge populations were virtually wiped out from the mid-1800's to the early 1900's. Settlers hunted the birds and destroyed their nesting *habitats* (living places) with *agricultural developments* (farmland). The number of cranes reached a low point during the winter of 1941-1942, when only about 15 birds were seen in Texas and another 6 in Louisiana.

Reproduction. Most whooping cranes today breed in marshland at Wood Buffalo National Park in Canada's Northwest Territories, where females typically lay two eggs in a nest made of plant material. Each year, the Wood Buffalo whooping cranes migrate more than 2,480 miles (4,000 kilometers) to Aransas National Wildlife Refuge in Texas for the winter. As the days grow longer at the start of spring, the restless cranes begin dancing and calling to each other before flying back north. Mated pairs return to the same nesting site year after year.

Conservation. In a desperate attempt to save the *species* (type), biologists placed 289 whooping crane eggs in the nests of sandhill cranes in Grays Lake National Wildlife Refuge in Idaho during the 1970's and 1980's. The sandhill cranes *incubated* the eggs (kept them warm, so they would hatch) and raised the young whoopers. Although many of these whoopers

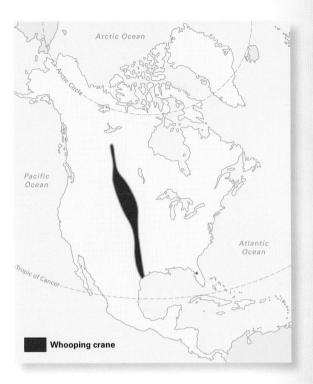

Whooping crane

survived to adulthood, they would not mate with each other. In the 1990's, scientists began releasing whooping cranes born in captivity into the wild at Kissimmee Prairie in Florida.

Biologists began another creative conservation effort in the autumn of 2001. The scientists dressed in big whooping crane costumes and used a small white airplane to lead a group of captive-born cranes from Wisconsin's Necedah National Wildlife Refuge to Florida's Chassahowitzka National Wildlife Refuge. The cranes followed the plane containing the strangely dressed people like they would follow a parent bird. The following spring, the cranes returned to Wisconsin by themselves. The biologists repeated this autumn migration several more years with the birds, and the cranes eventually started breeding in Wisconsin.

Thanks to the imaginative help of conservationists, whooping crane numbers have increased to several hundred birds in the wild, with more than 100 in captivity. Although it is still an endangered species, the whooping crane represents one of the greatest conservation success stories in North America.

Thanks to the imaginative help of conservationists, whooping crane numbers have increased to several hundred.

Campephilus principalis

Conservation status: Critically Endangered
(IUCN) Endangered (USFWS)

One of the largest—and rarest—woodpeckers
in the world, the ivory-billed woodpecker is
either critically endangered or extinct. The last
confirmed sighting of this *species* (type) in the
United States was in the 1940's, when the woodpecker was spotted in northeastern Louisiana.
Scientists believe the species may have last
been seen in Cuba in the 1980's.

Habitat and threats. The ivory-billed woodpecker was once common in swampy forests
throughout the southeastern United States.
It ranged from Florida northward to North
Carolina and southern Illinois and westward to
southeastern Oklahoma and eastern Texas. It
also lived in Cuba. However, decades of logging,
mining, and other disturbances of its forest
habitat (living place) caused the ivory-billed
woodpecker to disappear. Some people hunted
the woodpeckers.

Since 2004, several people have reported
seeing ivory-billed woodpeckers in the wild, but
scientists disagree about the *reliability* (depend-
ability) of those reports. Some of these people
have made sound and video recordings of what
they claim are ivory-billed woodpeckers in Arkansas, Florida, and elsewhere. There are some
scientists who believe that this evidence proves
that the species still exists, most likely in small,
isolated populations. Yet other scientists remain
unconvinced.

Species. One possible problem with the reported sightings is that a similar species, called the
pileated woodpecker, lives in part of the histori-
cal *range* (natural area) of the ivory-billed woodpecker. So some people may have actually seen
the much more common pileated woodpecker.

Both the ivory-billed and pileated woodpecker males are black-and-white birds with a
bright red crest on their head. Females lack this
crest. The ivory-billed species is larger than the

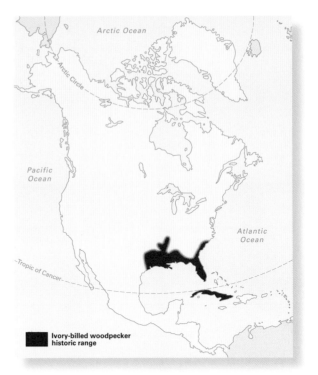

Ivory-billed woodpecker
historic range

pileated species, measuring from 18 to 20 inches (46 to 51 centimeters) in length. Ivory-billed
and pileated woodpeckers also differ in their
calls. Ivory-billed woodpeckers make a nasal
"yank" call that sounds something like a toy
tin trumpet, while pileated woodpeckers make
a deeper "kuk" call. And the two species make
different drumming noises when they peck
on trees. An ivory-billed woodpecker makes a
loud, strong "double-rap" sound as it pecks. It
can peck out a hole 4.7 inches (12 centimeters)
deep in less than a minute as it tries to reach
grubs inside a tree.

Conservation. Scientists are working hard
to protect the forest areas where ivory-billed
woodpecker sightings have been made since
2004. If the species truly does still exist, conservationists want to make sure that it can
hang on permanently.

**A 19th-century hand-colored etching of an
ivory-billed woodpecker. The bird was once
common in swampy forests throughout the
Southeast.**

Eumops floridanus

Conservation status: Critically Endangered (IUCN) Endangered (USFWS)

Growing to a length of about 6.5 inches (16.5 centimeters), with a wingspan of 20 inches (51 centimeters), the Florida bonneted bat is the largest *species* (type) of bat in the "sunshine state." Other than its size, there is little about the bat's appearance that makes it stand out. Its color ranges from rather drab shades of black to gray to brown. The Florida bonneted bat is an insect eater—preferring moths, mosquitoes, and other nighttime-flying insects.

Habitat. Florida bonneted bats live in southern Florida, mainly in the areas of Miami, Coral Gables, and Fort Lauderdale—all areas with large numbers of people. The bat's natural *habitat* (living place) consists of forests, where it roosts in *cavities* (open spaces) in old trees. More and more of its forest habitat has been destroyed as the human population of southern Florida has exploded.

However, Florida bonneted bats do not restrict themselves to natural areas. Many of these bats are comfortable roosting on the Spanish tile roofs that are so popular on southern Florida houses. Many bats also use special artificial roosts, called bat houses, that conservationists have built for them.

Although this species of bat can easily use human-built structures for roosting sites, many

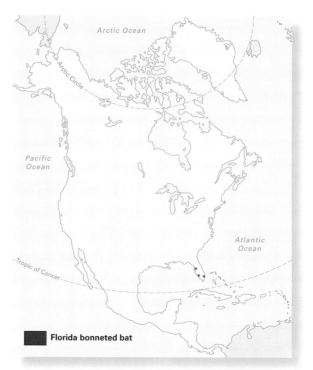

Florida bonneted bat

old buildings with spaces suitable for roosting have been torn down. This is a second kind of habitat loss—just as harmful to the bat populations as loss of their natural forest habitat.

Reproduction. Female Florida bonneted bats can give birth to only one or two young per year. One birth may occur in summer and another in winter in the bat's warm southern habitat. However, not all females reproduce twice each year. Many other kinds of bats also have only one or two young per year, though some

A Florida professor (above) records sounds from Florida bonneted bats (left) that had taken up residence in a golf course.

species have more. The fewer young a species has, the more difficult it is for that species's population to recover from being endangered.

Threats. Besides the loss of its roosting sites, another serious threat to the Florida bonneted bat is the spraying of *toxic* (poisonous) chemical pesticides to kill mosquitoes. These chemical compounds are harmful to the bats in two

ways. The compounds kill an important food source of the bats, and the poisons may also cause diseases in the bats themselves. Severe hurricanes, which are common is southern Florida, pose a natural threat to the bats by killing old trees that offer good roosting cavities.

Conservation. Today, the total population of the Florida bonneted bat may be fewer than 250 adults. Biologists believe that this population may still be declining. They also believe that more research is needed to better understand the behaviors of this bat, the threats to the bat, and the best ways to protect the bat.

Cynomys parvidens

Conservation status: Endangered (IUCN)
Threatened (USFWS)

Along with the Mexican prairie dog (*C. mexicanus*), the Utah prairie dog is the most endangered of the five *species* (types) of prairie dogs. All of these species of burrowing rodent live in western North America. The Utah species is also the smallest, with adults averaging about 11 inches (29 centimeters) in length.

■ Utah prairie dog

Habitat. Prairie dogs are famous for their complex burrow systems, with some burrows dug as deep as 16 feet (5 meters). The animals live in these burrows in large groups called colonies or "prairie dog towns." A colony may contain more than 500 individuals. Most burrows are made with at least two entrances, each surrounded by a mound of soil. The high mounds help keep water out of the burrows during heavy rains and floods, and they also provide prairie dogs with perches to watch for predators. The many predators of these rodents include badgers, coyotes, ferrets, golden eagles, and prairie falcons. When a prairie dog sees a predator, it makes a loud warning call that sounds like a dog's bark. The animals of the colony retreat underground only if the predator comes near.

Prairie dogs sleep in their burrows at night. They come out of their burrows during the daytime to eat. They eat mainly grasses and other plant food. But they also sometimes eat grasshoppers and other insects.

The Utah prairie dog has disappeared from more than 90 percent of its original *range* (natural area). It now lives only in a small area of grassland in southern Utah. Two other species of prairie dog—Gunnison's prairie dog and the white-tailed prairie dog—have larger ranges in nearby areas.

Threats. Most prairie dog populations shrank during the 1900's as ranchers killed vast numbers of the rodents and also destroyed their grassland *habitats* (living places) with farms, grazing, roads, and *urban* (city) developments. The ranchers killed the prairie dogs by poisoning and shooting, because they feared their livestock would step into burrows and injure their legs. They also wanted to stop the prairie dogs from eating the grasses preferred by cattle— even though the rodents and the cattle actually eat different types of plants. Moreover, grazing by cattle led to changes in the grassland plant species, with sagebrush taking over from the grasses preferred by the prairie dogs. These vegetation changes harmed the prairie dog populations.

Frequent droughts in the western United States have further reduced the grass food resources of the prairie dogs. And an infectious disease called plague has added to the problems of these animals. Thus, despite conservation efforts and laws to protect the Utah prairie dog and its habitat, this species remains endangered.

The grasses that were the Utah prairie dog's main food supply as well as the rodent's habitat have been largely destroyed by cattle ranching.

Mustela nigripes

Conservation status: Endangered (IUCN & USFWS)

The fate of this predatory weasel of the North American Great Plains has long been linked to that of prairie dogs. As prairie dog populations were wiped out by ranchers who viewed the burrowing rodents as unwanted pests, the ferret population that depended on the prairie dogs for food also declined. The killing of the prairie dogs took away not only the ferrets' main food supply but also their shelters.

Black-footed ferrets are fast-moving, intelligent *carnivores* (meat eaters) with long, thin, muscular bodies. Wild ferrets look much like the domestic ferrets that some people keep as pets, though domestic ferrets are larger. The fur of both wild and domestic ferrets is mostly creamy yellow, with black feet, a black tail, and a "mask" of black fur around the eyes.

In addition to prairie dogs, ferrets may eat ground squirrels, mice, and voles during their nighttime hunts. The ferrets communicate by hissing and chattering within their group. They communicate signals about how *dominant* (high-ranking) they are by marking the land with their urine and feces. When they become frightened, they may release a strong-smelling fluid from scent glands under the tail—much like a skunk.

Habitat. Black-footed ferrets once lived throughout much of the Great Plains, from southern Canada to northern Mexico. They used prairie dog burrows for homes and hiding places during the day. When ranchers killed the prairie dogs, they often filled in the rodents' burrows because of the danger the deep burrows posed to livestock. Thus, black-footed ferrets became endangered along with prairie dogs. The prairie dog-ferret relationship is an example of how changes in the population of one *species* (type) can have far-reaching effects on other species in the same *ecosystem* (natural systems made up of living organisms and their physical environment).

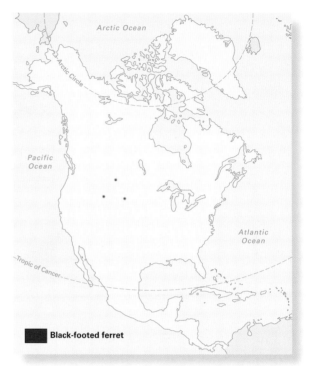

Black-footed ferret

Threats. The decline in the black-footed ferret population began in the late 1800's as ranchers began poisoning prairie dogs. The spread of a disease called distemper and the loss of natural grassland to agriculture further harmed the ferret populations. By the 1970's, many scientists thought that black-footed ferrets were extinct.

Conservation. In 1981, ranchers in Wyoming discovered a small population of the ferrets. Over the next several years, biologists captured all the wild ferrets to save them from distemper and other threats. Scientists then began breeding the ferrets in captivity. In 1991, they began releasing captive-born ferrets into western grasslands that had prairie dog populations. Today, wild black-footed ferrets live in a few small populations in northeastern Montana, western South Dakota, and southeastern Wyoming.

The black-footed ferret became endangered with the collapse of the prairie dog population on the Great Plains. The killing of the prairie dogs by ranchers took away the ferret's main food supply and shelter.

Gray wolf
Canis lupus

Conservation status: Least Concern (IUCN) Endangered, but main populations delisted (USFWS)

Mexican wolf
C. lupus baileyi

Conservation status: Proposed Endangered (USFWS)

Despite its common name, the gray wolf varies in color from pure white in the Arctic to jet black in Canadian subarctic forests. Many wolves are mixes of gray, brown, and black. Mexican wolves are a small-sized subspecies.

Wolves are well known for their intelligence and their social interaction in groups called packs. Each wolf pack is led by *dominant* wolves (high-ranking members). Biologists can identify a dominant wolf by its body language. When a dominant wolf meets a lower-ranking member of the pack, the top-ranking animal stands erect, holds its tail aloft, and points its ears up and forward.

Wolves and people have a complex relationship that goes back thousands of years. Although wolves have long been feared, the dogs we live with today are descended from wolves that people *domesticated* (tamed) about 14,000 years ago.

Habitat. The gray wolf once lived from the Arctic and subarctic regions of North America to the southern United States. Mexican wolves lived in the southwestern United States and Mexico.

Threats. Over the centuries, wolves have been hated by many people—especially farmers and ranchers, who feared wolves would kill their livestock or their family members. These attitudes led people to kill vast numbers of wolves—often with the help of government poisoning programs. By the mid-1900's, the only places in the lower 48 states of the United States where gray wolves could be found were northern Minnesota,

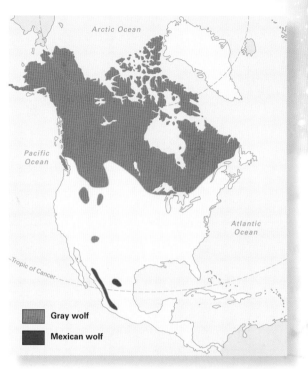

Gray wolf

Mexican wolf

Conservation efforts have led to the partial recovery of the gray wolf (right) population. Only an estimated 75 Mexican wolves (below) remain in the American Southwest.

Isle Royale in Lake Superior, and parts of the Southwest. In addition, the red wolf (a separate, smaller-sized species) was found along the Gulf coasts of Texas and Louisiana. And many thousands of grays still lived in Canada and Alaska.

Conservation. Since the early 1970's, legal protections under the Endangered Species Act (ESA) have brought back the gray wolf. Some wolves from Canada moved to the United States to *recolonize* (live again in) previous wolf *habitats* (living places). Other wolves were reintroduced into protected areas in the United States by scientists. Since the 1990's, many gray wolves have been successfully released in the Yellowstone National Park *ecosystem*, which covers parts of Idaho, Montana, and Wyoming. Mexican wolves have been released in parts of Arizona and New Mexico as an "Experimental" population by the USFWS. (An ecosystem is a group of animals and the environment they live in.)

In the early 2000's, the recovery of wolf populations led the USFWS to "delist" gray wolves in their two main home regions in the lower 48 states—the Western Great Lakes region (Michigan, Minnesota, and Wisconsin) and the Northern Rocky Mountains region (Idaho, Montana, and Wyoming). More than 5,000 wolves now live in those two regions. (Wolves also have spread into Washington State and Oregon.) The "delisting" removed federal protection for these wolf populations under the ESA. But the wolf populations are still managed by the states to make sure they stay at healthy numbers. Despite the delisting, the species as a whole remained classified by the USFWS as "Endangered" in the lower 48 states as of early 2014.

Roughly 75 Mexican wolves make up the small population in the southwest United States. The USFWS has proposed changing the "Experimental" status of this subspecies population to "Endangered" to give it greater protection.

Canis rufus

Conservation status: Critically Endangered (IUCN) Endangered (USFWS)

The red wolf is one of the world's most endangered *species* (type) of *canid* (member of the dog family). By 1980, there were no wild red wolves in North America, and only 14 survived in captivity. Thanks to a captive-breeding program and releases of wolves from this program, a very small population of wild red wolves has been reestablished in North Carolina.

Red wolves have smaller, more coyote-like bodies than gray wolves, with longer legs and shorter fur. The red wolf's fur is mostly a tawny reddish color sprinkled with gray and black. Like gray wolves, red wolves live in packs.

Each pack has a *dominant* (high-ranking) male and female that mate for life. They build their den in a burrow in a field or stream bank, among thick plant growth, or in empty spaces of large old trees. The female gives birth to a litter of three to eight pups. Both parents raise the young, often with help from the other pack members. The young wolves go off on their own when they are from 15 to 20 months old. At that point, they are able to capture prey on their own, mainly rabbits, raccoons, and deer.

Habitat. The red wolf once lived throughout the southeastern United States, up the eastern seaboard to New England, and westward to Texas.

Threats. Red wolves were killed off by people for the same reasons that gray wolves were exterminated. Those reasons included fears among farmers and other people that the wolves would kill their livestock or family members. Throughout history, people have also viewed wolves as competitors for living space and game animals. Such attitudes played roles in the killing of both red and gray wolves in the United States.

Conservation. After the red wolf species disappeared from the wild in 1980, scientists with

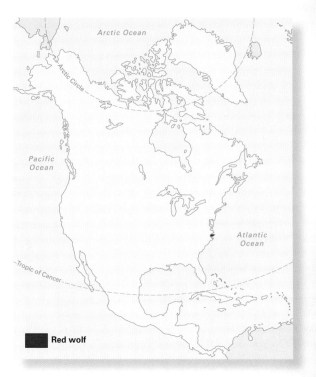

Red wolf

the USFWS and 40 wildlife facilities began to breed these canids in captivity. The scientists began releasing some of these captive-born red wolves into the wild in 1987. An "experimental" population of red wolves was set up at the Alligator River National Wildlife Refuge in North Carolina and nearby areas. Only wolves that had successfully bred with each other were released. There are now more than 150 red wolves in about 20 packs living in their natural *habitat* (living place) in North Carolina. There are also about 200 red wolves in captivity.

Biologists with the USFWS hope to build up red wolf numbers to about 550, including at least 220 animals in the wild. However, red wolves tend to interbreed with coyotes, producing *hybrid* (mixed) animals rather than pure red wolves. This hybridization is a serious threat to the survival of the red wolf as a pure species.

The USFWS has reintroduced the red wolf at the Alligator River National Wildlife refuge in northeastern North Carolina.

Vulpes macrotis mutica

Conservation status: Endangered (USFWS)

Kit foxes are long-legged, skinny foxes with very large pointed ears and a very bushy tail. They are smaller than most foxes, ranging from 15 to 20 inches (38 to 52 centimeters) in length—not counting their tail, which may be as long as 13 inches (32 centimeters).

Species. Kit foxes do not sit or relax much. They move around a lot, busily running back and forth while keeping a lookout for danger, such as coyotes and other predators. They can run as fast as 25 miles (40 kilometers) per hour, at least for short distances. Considering their speediness, it makes sense that they are closely related to another type of fox called the swift fox. Swift foxes live mainly in grasslands east of the Rocky Mountains. But the *ranges* (natural areas) of the kit and swift foxes overlap somewhat. The two *species* (types) sometimes interbreed and produce *hybrid* (mixed) offspring.

Habitat. Kit foxes live mainly in hot deserts and semidesert areas in the southwestern United States and northern Mexico. Some live farther north or farther east.

The bodies of kit foxes have special traits—or *adaptations*—for living in the desert. Their big ears release heat from the body, helping them to stay cool. A lot of fur grows between the fleshy pads at the bottom of their feet. This extra fur helps the foxes walk on the hot sand without burning their feet. The fur also helps the feet get *traction* (ability to pull against a surface) on the loose sand.

Threats. Throughout its range in the West, the populations of kit foxes vary in size depending on the exact location. For the species's population as a whole, most biologists believe that it is stable and safe. The IUCN classifies the kit fox as being of "Least Concern" in terms of its conservation status. However, the population in the San Joaquin Valley of California is classified as

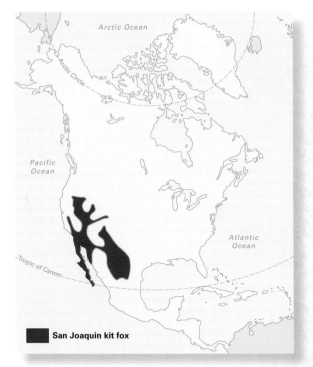

San Joaquin kit fox

"Endangered" by the USFWS. The main cause of this classification is the spread of agriculture, cities, roads, and industries throughout that region.

All the human developments in the San Joaquin Valley have broken up and destroyed the natural *habitat* (living place) of the kit fox. These foxes cannot survive when their desert environment—to which they are specially adapted—is changed into irrigated croplands or oil fields. The endangered status of the San Joaquin kit fox serves as a good example of how important a healthy, natural habitat is to the survival of a species.

The population of San Joaquin kit foxes has also been harmed by the poisoning of their prey, such as prairie dogs, by farmers and ranchers. The loss of this prey has made it harder for the foxes to find food. In Mexico, the kit foxes are sometimes captured and sold as pets.

In California's San Joaquin Valley, the kit fox has become endangered due to human development, particularly agriculture and industry.

Urocyon littoralis

Conservation status: Near Threatened (IUCN)

Like the kit fox, the island fox is another small North American *canid* (member of the dog family). Biologists point to the island fox as an example of how evolution works. They believe that the island fox is a descendant of the gray fox, a large canid that lives in much of North America.

Habitat. Some gray foxes migrated to the Channel Islands, off the coast of southern California, more than 10,000 years ago. Scientists think that those foxes either swam to the islands or rode some floating plant debris there. After arriving on the islands, their bodies changed over the course of several *generations* (all members of a species born in the same general time period). They became smaller from one generation to the next.

According to biologists, this so-called "dwarfism" often happens to a *species* (type) when it moves to an island. The island usually has fewer food resources than the larger mainland from which the species came. So it benefits the species to have smaller bodies, which need less food. The island may also have fewer predators than the mainland, so the species does not have to be large to protect itself. Eventually the island foxes changed enough that they became a different species from the mainland gray foxes. An island fox is only about one-half to two-thirds the size of a gray fox.

Threats. Many years ago, few daytime predators bothered the foxes on the six Channel Islands where they live. Because of the lack of predator threats, the island foxes were more likely than gray foxes to be active during the day. However, golden eagles became attracted to the Channel Islands in the 1990's after people brought wild pigs to the islands. Today, these large birds of prey are a major threat to the foxes.

Island foxes face many other threats caused by human activities. Cats brought to the islands by people capture the same kind of rodents and

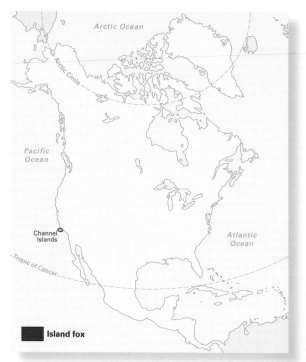

Island fox

other small prey that the foxes need for food. Canine distemper and other diseases from domestic dogs sometimes spread to the foxes, weakening or killing the wild animals. Roads, buildings, and other human developments disrupt or destroy the foxes' *habitat* (living place). Many foxes end up becoming roadkill as they try to move from one isolated piece of grassland or forest to another isolated piece.

Even scientists are to blame for some of the island foxes' problems. In 1999 and 2000, scientists purposely killed some island foxes—and removed others from their habitat—because they feared the foxes were a threat to an endangered species of bird called the loggerhead shrike.

The fox population on some islands has become so reduced that biologists now fear any additional problem—such as another dog disease or a severe weather event—could completely wipe out the species.

After living for several generations on small islands off the coast of California, the island fox became a distinct new species, smaller than mainland foxes.

Gulf Coast jaguarundi

Puma (Herpailurus) yagouaroundi cacomitli

Conservation status: Endangered (USFWS)

Sinaloan jaguarundi

Puma (Herpailurus) yagouaroundi tolteca

Conservation status: Endangered (USFWS)

These two endangered cats are the North American subspecies of the jaguarundi, a cat that looks a little like a weasel or an otter, with a long neck, short ears, stubby legs, and long tail. Some people call them "otter cats." Jaguarundis are about 1 foot (30 centimeters) tall at the shoulders and from 3 to 4 feet (91 to 122 centimeters) long. They range in color from reddish-yellow to grayish-brown to black. Cats with lighter colors usually live in open areas, while those with darker colors typically live in forests.

Habitats. The Gulf Coast and Sinaloan subspecies live mainly in thick brushlands in the Rio Grande Valley of Texas. They can also be found along the western coast of Mexico. Other jaguarundi subspecies live in Central and South America.

Diet. Jaguarundis hunt and eat armadillos, rabbits, rodents, and occasionally chickens or other farm animals. They'll sometimes jump into the air to catch birds flying close to the ground. They are also good swimmers, and they'll often go into water to capture fish or other aquatic prey.

Reproduction. Males and females come together sometime in the autumn to mate. The female usually gives birth to 1 or 2 kittens in a den inside a hollow log, a thicket of plants, or some other shelter. The kittens may stay with the mother for two years.

Each subspecies of jaguarundi has several unique calls that it makes for particular

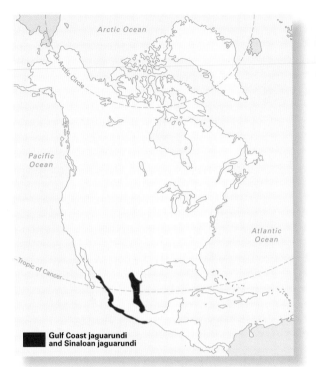

Gulf Coast jaguarundi and Sinaloan jaguarundi

reasons. Some calls are made only during mating, others during friendly encounters, others when feeling threatened, and still others occur just between mothers and kittens.

Threats. The destruction of *habitat* (living place) has caused the populations of Gulf Coast and Sinaloan jaguarundis to become endangered. This habitat destruction is mainly the result of the growing human population in the Rio Grande Valley. As people replace the natural brushland with farmland, houses, businesses, and roads, fewer and fewer wild cats can survive. As their natural prey becomes more difficult to find, the jaguarundis turn more to farm animals. Farmers then killed the cats. The pelts of jaguarundis are not highly desired, but the cats are sometimes killed in traps meant for more valued fur-bearing animals, such as beavers.

Conservation. Scientists are working to restore destroyed habitat in the Rio Grande Valley by replanting native shrubs.

A jaguarundi prowls through its native habitat in the Rio Grande Valley of Texas. Both the Gulf Coast and Sinaloan subspecies are endangered due to habitat destruction.

Tapirus bairdii

Conservation status: Endangered (IUCN & USFWS)

Tapirs are unusual piglike animals that have what looks like the stub of an elephant's trunk. But these animals are actually related to horses. Fossil evidence shows that tapirs have remained almost unchanged for the past 35 million years. Today, different *species* (types) of tapirs live in Central America, South America, and Asia.

Appearance. The two Central American species of tapirs are the smallest members of the tapir family, though the largest mammals native to Central America. Their bodies are about 6.5 feet (2 meters) long and 4 feet (1.2 meters) high at the shoulders. They can weigh as much as 880 pounds (400 kilograms).

Like all tapirs, the Baird's tapir has a heavy, barrel-shaped body with a thick neck, and its long nose and upper lip are formed into a short, movable *proboscis* (snout). Adult Baird's tapirs have mostly dark brown fur, with yellowish throat and cheeks.

Habitat. Baird's tapirs are rather mysterious creatures. They typically live deep in the forest, and they shy away from contact with people. They usually live near streams or other bodies of water, and when they get frightened, they often run into the water to hide. They are good swimmers and can briefly stay underwater.

Diet. Scientists believe that Baird's tapirs feed on the twigs and leaves of trees and shrubs, as well as on fruits and seeds. They often feed during the night in forest clearings. The tapirs live in male-and-female pairs or in small family groups. They make high-pitched whistling calls to communicate with each other.

Reproduction. Females are thought to give birth to only a single young at a time. The young tapir may stay with its mother for two years. Only after that can the mother reproduce again.

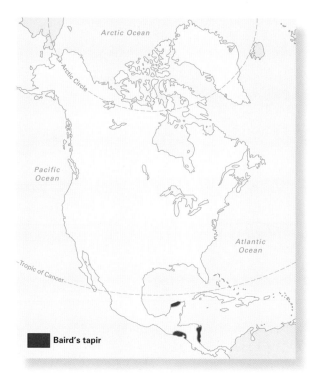

Baird's tapir

Threats. Baird's tapirs used to be common in natural areas throughout Central America, from southern Mexico through Panama and into northern Colombia. Today, the tapirs occur in populations that are very fragmented—meaning that small groups live in natural *habitats* (living places) that are widely separated from other natural habitats by some-times large areas of human developments. According to some scientific estimates, 70 percent of the forests in Central America have been destroyed since the 1970's because of human activities.

Tapirs face other threats besides the loss of their habitat. Some people in Central America hunt tapirs for their meat or for sport. Fatal diseases from horses and cattle have spread into tapir populations.

Conservation. The tapirs are protected by laws in most Central American nations, but those laws are often not enforced. Even if Baird's tapirs are perfectly protected, their slow reproductive rate will make it difficult for this species's population to recover.

The original habitat of the Baird's tapir was the rain forests of Central America. Its population has dwindled with the loss of this habitat because of human development.

Ursus arctos horribilis

Conservation status: Threatened (USFWS)
Vulnerable (COSEWIC)

Grizzly bears are a subspecies of brown bear found in much of Alaska and western Canada, as well as in parts of Washington, Idaho, Montana, and Wyoming. A grizzly bear may be as long as 8 feet (2.4 meters), with a large hump on its shoulders. The hump marks a place where powerful muscles are attached, giving the bear great strength to dig dens. Adult males weigh as much as 600 pounds (270 kilograms) and females as much as 400 pounds (180 kilograms). The *underfur* (lower layer of fur beneath the outer layer) of grizzly bears is thick, woolly, and brownish or blackish. Their outer fur is tipped with white or silver, making the bears look a bit grizzled, that is, grayish.

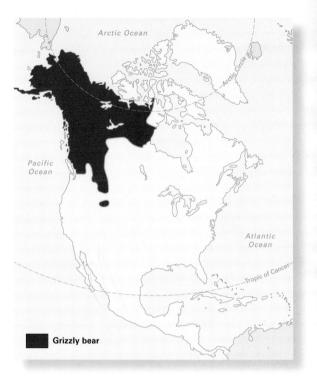

Grizzly bear

Diet. Most of a grizzly bear's diet consists of plant food, including nuts, seeds, berries, leaves, roots, and grasses. They also catch and eat insects, fish, and mammals, such as ground squirrels and young elk. But they get most of their meat from eating *carcasses* (dead bodies of animals). A large grizzly may eat as much as 90 pounds (40 kilograms) of food in a single day.

Hibernation. During the winter, grizzly bears hibernate in dens inside caves, in holes dug into the ground, or in other shelters. During hibernation, their heart rate slows, their body temperature drops, and they survive on stored fat reserves. But the bears will wake up if disturbed. In addition, females give birth to one or two cubs in January or February and nurse them inside the den. The cubs come out of the den with the mother in spring. They may stay with her for three years. Most grizzly bears try to avoid contact with people.

Habitat and threats. In the early 1800's, tens of thousands of grizzly bears lived in western North America. Then people began destroying the grizzly's natural prairie, woodland, and forest *habitats* (living places) by clearing the land for settlements, farms, roads, logging, and other purposes. People also put out forest fires—which was bad for the bears. Regular wildfires helped add nutrients to the soil and helped increase the spread of shrubs that the grizzlies preferred to eat.

Grizzlies seldom damage cabins and campsites or prey on livestock. On very rare occasions, they may attack humans.

Conservation. Today, laws in the United States and Canada protect grizzly bears, and their populations are recovering. In 2007, biologists determined that the grizzly population near Yellowstone National Park had recovered so well that it no longer needed special U.S. protection.

Before the widespread settling of the West in the 1800's, there were as many as 50,000 grizzly bears living in the United States from the Great Plains to the Pacific Coast.

Polar bear

Ursus maritimus

Conservation status: Vulnerable (IUCN) Threatened (USFWS) Vulnerable (COSEWIC)

An adult male polar bear may be as long as 8.5 feet (2.6 meters) and as heavy as 1,300 pounds (590 kilograms). Females are much smaller. A polar bear has an especially long neck with a narrow head, sharp teeth, and sharp curved claws.

Habitat. Polar bears are built for extreme cold. Their thick fur and the layers of fat beneath their skin keep them warm in their Arctic homes in the ice-covered waters off the northern coasts of Alaska, Canada, Greenland, Norway, and Russia. The big white bears live as far north as the North Pole, and they may stay active all winter. However, even polar bears will hide inside dens during the worst winter weather.

Polar bears can spend a lot of time in the water because they are great swimmers, capable of paddling for long distances with their front paws. On the land, they can run as fast as 25 miles (40 kilometers) an hour.

Diet. The polar bear body is perfectly adapted for hunting its main prey—ringed seals and bearded seals. The bears usually hunt the seals by grabbing them when they come up for air through holes in the sea ice or by pouncing on the seals as they rest on *ice floes* (floating chunks of ice). The bears will also sometimes kill young seals right at the seals' snowy dens on the land. Polar bears also eat berries and grasses, seaweed, birds' eggs, ducks, geese, lemmings, reindeer, and walrus. Some polar bears eat other polar bears.

Threats. The icy, polar *habitat* (living place) of polar bears is threatened by a number of problems. Scientists believe the most serious problem is global warming, which has reduced the amount of sea ice in the Arctic. As long as polar bears have access to sea ice, they can hunt

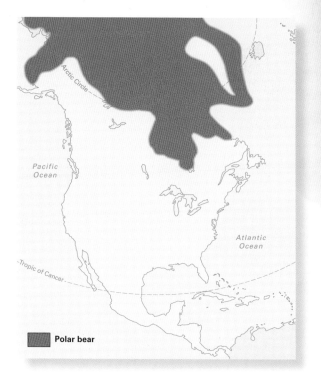

Polar bear

successfully in the ocean for seals, their most important food source. However, if the sea ice melts completely during the summer, polar bears may be forced to use the limited, less preferred food resources on land. They may even be forced to spend several months living off of their stored fat reserves. Scientists fear that continued global warming will cause such a loss of all summertime sea ice in the Arctic.

Another threat to the bears' survival is pollution of Arctic *ecosystems* with industrial chemicals, including compounds called PCB's and dioxins. (An ecosystem is a group of animals and their physical environment.) Such chemicals, which flow to the Arctic in water and wind currents from places farther south, harm the bears' immune systems and other body functions. In addition, traditional hunting of polar bears by Inuit people may be more than the polar bear population can withstand at this point.

Scientists believe the most serious problem facing polar bears is global warming, which has reduced the amount of sea ice in the Arctic.

44

Glossary

Aboriginal Refers to the earliest people present in a region and their descendants.

Adaptation A trait that makes an animal better able to survive in its environment.

Agricultural development The replacing of natural land with farmland.

Arboreal Living in or among trees.

Brackish Partially salty water.

Canid A member of the dog family, such as a coyote, fox, or wolf.

Carapace Shell or other hard covering on the back of such animals as tortoises.

Carcass A dead body.

Carnivore An animal that eats mainly meat.

Carrion The remains of dead animals.

Cavity An open space.

Climate change Long-term changes in the climate believed to be caused by the burning of fossil fuels.

Domesticate To tame.

Dominant In terms of animal behavior, refers to a powerful individual who influences the behavior of other individuals.

Ecosystem A natural system made up of the living organisms and the physical environment in a region.

Feral Refers to domestic animals that escaped into the wild.

Generation All the members of a species born in the same general time period.

Habitat The type of environment in which an organism usually lives.

Hybrid Offspring produced by the mating of two different species.

Ice floe Floating chunks of ice.

Incubate To sit on eggs, cover them with vegetation, or keep them warm in other ways so that they will hatch.

Invertebrate An animal without a backbone, or spine.

Larvae Immature forms of some insects and other animals.

Proboscis Snout.

Range The area in which certain plants or animals live or naturally occur.

Recolonize Refers to a species once more living in an area that they had occupied but subsequently abandoned.

Reliability Being able to trust or depend on something or someone.

Sediment Loose dirt.

Silt Tiny pieces of sand, clay, or other matter carried by moving water.

Spawn Refers to the production of eggs by fish, frogs, shellfish, and other aquatic animals.

Species A group of animals or plants that have certain permanent characteristics in common and are able to interbreed.

Toxic Poisonous.

Traction Ability to pull against a surface.

Turbid Water that it is cloudy and murky with silt.

Underfur Lower layer of fur beneath the outer layer.

Urban Of or having to do with cities.

Urbanization The growth and spread of cities.

Urohydrosis Method by which certain birds cool themselves by urinating on their own legs.

Viviparous Reproducing by bringing forth live young, rather than eggs.

Books

Carson, Mary K., Tom Uhlman, and Merlin D. Tuttle. *The Bat Scientists*. Boston: Houghton Mifflin Books for Children, 2010. Print.

Frydenborg, Kay. *Wild Horse Scientists*. Boston: Houghton Mifflin Harcourt, 2012. Print.

Hammond, Paula. *The Atlas of Endangered Animals: Wildlife Under Threat Around the World*. Tarrytown, NY: Marshall Cavendish, 2010. Print.

Hoare, Ben, and Tom Jackson. *Endangered Animals*. New York: DK Pub., 2010. Print.

Silhol, Sandrine, Gaëlle Guérive, and Marie Doucedame. *Extraordinary Endangered Animals*. New York: Abrams Books for Young Readers, 2011. Print.

Websites

Arkive. Wildscreen, 2014. Web. 14 May 2014.

"Endangered Animals of the Americas." *National Geographic Education*. National Geographic Society, 2014. Web. 14 May 2014.

"Especies Fact Sheets." *Kids' Planet*. Defenders of Wildlife, n.d. Web. 14 May 2014.

"Save Our Species." *Pesticides: Endangered Species Protection Program*. U.S. Environmental Protection Agency, 2012. Web. 14 May 2014.

U.S. Fish & Wildlife Service Endangered Species. U.S. Fish & Wildlife Service, n.d. Web. 14 May 2014.

Tregaskis, Shiona. "The world's extinct and endangered species – interactive map." *The Guardian*. Guardian News and Media Limited, 3 Sept. 2012. Web. 14 May 2014.

Organizations *for helping endangered animals*

Alaska Wildlife Adoption
By adopting an animal at the Alaska Wildlife Conservation Center, you can enjoy animal parenthood without all the work.
http://www.alaskawildlife.org/support/alaska-wildlife-adoption/

Defenders of Wildlife
Founded in 1947, Defenders of Wildlife is a major national conservation organization focused on wildlife and habitat conservation.
http://www.defenders.org/take-action

National Geographic – Big Cats Initiative
National Geographic, along with Dereck and Beverly Joubert, launched the Big Cats Initiative to raise awareness and implement change to the dire situation facing big cats.
http://animals.nationalgeographic.com/animals/big-cats-initiative/

National Geographic – The Ocean Initiative
National Geographic's Ocean Initiative helps identify and support individuals and organizations that are using creative and entrepreneurial approaches to marine conservation.
http://ocean.nationalgeographic.com/ocean/about-ocean-initiative

National Wildlife Federation – Adoption Center
Symbolically adopt your favorite species and at the same time support the National Wildlife Federation's important work protecting wildlife and connecting people to nature.
http://www.shopnwf.org/Adoption-Center/index.cat

Neighbor Ape
Neighbor Ape strives to conserve the habitat of wild chimpanzees in southeastern Senegal, to protect the chimpanzees themselves, and to provide for the well-being of the Senegalese people who have traditionally lived in the area alongside these chimpanzees.
http://www.globalgiving.org/donate/10235/neighbor-ape/

Smithsonian National Zoo – Adopt a Species
The Adopt a Species program supports the National Zoo's extraordinary work in the conservation and care of the world's rarest animals.
http://nationalzoo.si.edu/support/adoptspecies/

World Wildlife Fund
World Wildlife Fund works in 100 countries and is supported by over 1 million members in the United States and close to 5 million globally.
http://www.worldwildlife.org/how-to-help

Index

Acknowledgments

The publishers acknowledge the following sources for illustrations. Credits read from top to bottom, left to right, on their respective pages. All maps, charts, and diagrams were prepared by the staff unless otherwise noted.

COVER: © Hannele Lahti, National Geographic/Getty Images; © Thomas Kitchin, Design Pics/Alamy Images
4 © Hannele Lahti, National Geographic/Getty Images
7 © USDA Photo/Alamy Images; © Craig Larcom, Alamy Images
8 © Visuals Unlimited/Nature Picture Library
11 © Mark Newman, Getty Images
13 © Minden/SuperStock; © Museum of Comparative Zoology, Harvard University
15 © Adrian Davies, Alamy Images; © Wayne Lynch, Getty Images
16-17 © Joel Sartore, National Geographic Society; © PureStock/Alamy Images
19 © John Cancalosi, Alamy Images

21 © William H. Mullins, Getty Images
23 © Jane Leaman, Alamy Images; © Alamy Images
25 © Patrick Farrell, Miami Herald/Alamy Images; © Joel Sartore, National Geographic/Getty Images
27 © Gerry Pearce, Alamy Images
29 © Wendy Shattil, Alamy Images
30-31 © Bob Gibbons, Alamy Images; © Tierfotoagentur/Alamy Images
33 © Bruce Coleman, Alamy Images
35-37 © Kevin Schafer, Alamy Images
39 © blickwinkel/Alamy Images
41 © Frans Lanting, Alamy Images
43 © John E. Marriott, SuperStock
45 © Martha Holmes, Nature Picture Library